Garden of Song

FEATURING TEXTS BY ROBERT LOUIS STEVENSON

10 Vocal Solos for Young Voices

Compiled and Edited by **Katie O'Connor-Ballantyne**

Access the audio online as well as on the Accompaniment CD.

Alfred Music
P.O. Box 10003
Van Nuys, CA 91410-0003
alfred.com

Book & Online Audio (00-48579)   ISBN-10: 1-4706-4321-9   ISBN-13: 978-1-4706-4321-8
Book (00-48580)   ISBN-10: 1-4706-4322-7   ISBN-13: 978-1-4706-4322-5
Online Audio (00-48581)
Accompaniment CD (00-48582)

1. COME, MY LITTLE CHILDREN

Words from A Child's Garland of Songs *by*
ROBERT LOUIS STEVENSON (1850-1894)

Music by
SALLY K. ALBRECHT

2-part choral arrangement available (41545).

15
ver - y small and clear, ver - y true to time and tune, and pleas-ing to the
20
ear.
21
mf
Come, my lit - tle chil - dren. Come, my lit - tle chil - dren.
mf
25
Come, my lit - tle chil - dren, here are songs for you.
30
33
mp
Mark the note that ris - es.
mp

Mark the notes that fall.
Mark the time when bro - ken, and the
swing of it all.
So when night is come, and you have gone to
bed, all the songs you love to sing shall ech - o in your head.
Come, my lit - tle chil - dren.
Come, my lit - tle chil - dren.
Come, my lit - tle

chil - dren,   here are songs for   you.
Come, my lit - tle   chil - dren.   Come, my lit - tle   chil - dren.   Come, my lit - tle
chil - dren,   here are songs for   you,   for
you,   for   you.
mf
mf
mp
mp
p
rit. e decresc.
p
rit. e decresc.
pp
8va

2. FOREIGN LANDS

Words from *A Child's Garden of Verses* by
ROBERT LOUIS STEVENSON (1850-1894)

Music by
KATIE O'CONNOR-BALLANTYNE

2-part choral arrangement available (43464).

who should climb but lit - tle me?___ I held the trunk with
both my hands,___ and looked a - broad in for - eign lands.___
18
mp
I saw the next door gar - den lie,___
mp
a-dorned with flow'rs be - fore my eye.___ And man - y pleas - ant

plac - es more___ that I had nev - er seen be -
fore. I saw the dim - pling
riv - er pass___ and be the sky's blue look - ing glass.___
The dust - y roads___ go up___ and down with

peo - ple tramp - ing in - to town.
If I could find a high - er tree,___ far - ther and far - ther
I should see,___ to where the grown - up riv - er slips,___
in - to the sea a - mong the ships,___ to

cresc.
where the roads on ei - ther hand lead on - ward in - to
mf cresc.
f
fair - y land,
mf
where all the chil - dren
dine at five, and all the play - things come a -
rit.
rit.
a tempo
poco rit.
live.
a tempo
decresc.
poco rit.
p

3. THE MOON HAS A FACE

Words from A Child's Garden of Verses *by*
ROBERT LOUIS STEVENSON (1850-1894)

Music and additional Words by
GLENDA E. FRANKLIN

2-part choral arrangement available (47194).

* pronounced "keys"

12
in the forks of the trees. The moon, the
moon, it shines so ver-y bright. The moon, the
moon, it lights the dark, the deep-est, dark-est night.
The squall-ing cat and the squeak-ing mouse, the howl-ing dog by the
mf
16
cresc.
mf
p
poco rit.
poco rit.
p
a tempo
mp
25
a tempo
mp

28
30
p
door of the house, the bat that lies in bed at noon, all
32
mf
love to be out by the light of the moon. The
cresc.
36
moon, the moon, it shines so ver - y bright. The
mf
40
p poco rit.
moon, the moon, it lights the dark, the deep-est, dark-est night.
poco rit.
p

a tempo
mp
45
But all of the things that be - long to the day cud - dle to sleep to be
48
50
out of her way; and flow-ers and chil - dren close their eyes till
p
52
up in the morn - ing, the sun shall a - rise, the sun shall a -
mp
56
rise, the sun shall a - rise!
mf
cresc.
f

4. MY SHADOW

Words from A Child's Garden of Verses *by*
ROBERT LOUIS STEVENSON (1850-1894)

Music by
DAVE *and* **JEAN PERRY**

2-part choral arrangement available (23579).

jump in - to my bed.
The
fun-ni-est thing a - bout him is the way he likes to grow, not at all like prop - er chil-dren, which is
al - ways ver - y slow; for he some-times shoots up tall - er like an In-di-a rub - ber ball,
and he some-times gets so lit - tle that there's none of him at all.

He has-n't got a no - tion of how chil-dren ought to
play, and can on - ly make a fool of me in ev - 'ry sort of
way. He stays so close be-side me, he's a cow - ard you can see, I'd think
shame to stick to nurs - ie as that shad - ow sticks to me! One
rit.
a tempo
mp
rit. e decresc.
mp
a tempo

41
morn-ing ver-y ear - ly be-fore the sun was up, I rose and found the shin-ing dew on
44
cresc.
rit.
ev -'ry but-ter-cup; but my la-zy lit-tle shad-ow, like an ar-rant sleep-y-head,
cresc.
rit.
47
a tempo
mf
had stayed at home, at home be-hind, had
(the alarm)
a tempo
mf
50
f
p
stayed at home be-hind me and was fast a-sleep in bed.
f
mf
p
subito
f

5. PIRATE STORY

Words from A Child's Garden of Verses *by*
ROBERT LOUIS STEVENSON (1850-1894)

Music and additional Words by
KATIE O'CONNOR-BALLANTYNE

2-part choral arrangement available (43601).

Winds are in the air, they are blow-ing in the spring, and waves are on the mead-ow like the
waves there are at sea.
Where shall we ad-ven-ture, to-day that we're a-float, war-y of the weath-er and
steer-ing by a star? Shall it be to Af-ri-ca, a-steer-ing of the boat, to

Prov - i - dence, or Bab - y - lon, or off to Mal - a - bar?
Hi! But here's a squad - ron a - row - ing on the sea. Cat - tle on the mead - ow a -
charg - ing with a roar! Quick, and we'll es - cape, they're as mad as they can be, the

wick - et is the har - bor and the gar - den is the shore.
Where shall we ad - ven - ture, to - day that we're a - float, war - y of the
weath - er and steer - ing by a star? Shall it be to Af - ri - ca, a - steer - ing of the
boat, to Prov - i - dence, or Bab - y - lon, or off to Mal - a - bar?

Where shall we ad - ven - ture, to - day that we're a - float, war - y of the
weath - er and steer - ing by a star? Shall it be to Af - ri - ca, a - steer - ing of the
boat, to Prov - i - dence, or Bab - y - lon, or
off to Mal - a - bar?

6. STAR DANCE

Words from A Child's Garden of Verses *by*
ROBERT LOUIS STEVENSON (1850-1894)

Music and additional Words by
JANET GARDNER

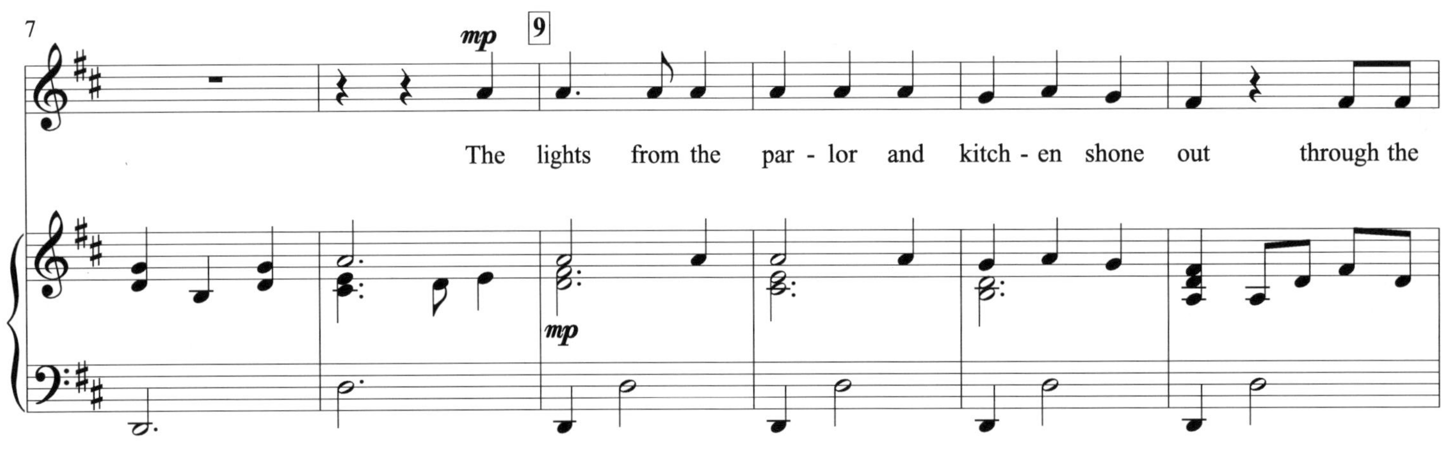

2-part choral arrangement available (38284).

19
mov - ing a - bout, there were thou - sands of mil - lions of stars._______ There
25
ne'er were such thou - sands of leaves on a tree, nor of peo - ple in church or the
31
33
park,______________ as the crowds of the stars that looked down up - on me, and that
37
41
mf
glit - tered and winked in the dark.____________ Stars, stars
cresc.
mf

26
43
shin - ing from a - far, smile on me to - night.
49
Dance, dance, shim - mer, and prance till the morn - ing
55
light.
decresc.
61
mp
63
The Dog, and the Plough, and the Hunt - er, and all, and the
mp

star of the sail - or, and Mars, these shone in the sky, and the
pail by the wall would be half full of wa - ter and stars. They
saw me at last, and they chased me with cries, and they soon had me packed in - to
bed. But the glo - ry kept shin - ing and bright in my eyes, and the

stars go-ing 'round in my head. Mil - lions of stars in the
heav - ens a - far, glim - mer-ing in the night,
danc - ing and pranc - ing as if in a trance. Oh, what a glo - ri - ous
sight. Stars, stars shin - ing from a - far,

smile on me to - night. Dance, dance,
shim - mer, and prance till the morn - ing light.
till the morn - ing light. What a
sight, glo - ri - ous light.

7. THE SWING

Words from A Child's Garden of Verses *by*
ROBERT LOUIS STEVENSON (1850-1894)

Music by
GREG GILPIN

2-part choral arrangement available (39736).

Up in the air, o - ver the wall, till I can see so wide,
riv - er and trees and cat - tle and all o - ver the coun - try -
side.
How do you like to go up in a swing, up in the air so blue?

Oh, I do think it the pleas - ant - est thing ev - er a child can do.
Up in the air, o - ver the wall, till I can see so
wide, riv - er and trees and cat - tle and all o - ver the coun - try -
side. Till I look down on the gar - den green,

46 Tempo I (♩. = ca. 56)
44
mf
mf
down on the roof so brown,___ up in the air I go fly - ing a - gain,
48
up in the air, up in the air, up in the air___ and
52
decresc.
mp
down!___ How do you like to go up in a swing,___
decresc.
mp
56
cresc.
mf f
up in a swing?___
cresc.
mf f mp

8. THIS SHALL BE FOR MUSIC

Words from "Romance" by
ROBERT LOUIS STEVENSON (1850-1894)

Music and additional Words by
MARY DONNELLY
and **GEORGE L. O. STRID**

2-part choral arrangement available (38003).

* Brooches (*broh-chehz*) - pieces of jewelry, usually fastened to clothing with a hinged pin and catch.

I will make a pal - ace fit for you and me, of green days in
for - ests and blue days at sea. And this shall be for mu - sic when
no one else is near, the fine song for sing - ing, the rare song to
hear. That on - ly I re - mem - ber, that on - ly you ad -
cresc.
mf
cresc.
mf
decresc.
decresc.

32
mp
mire, of the broad road be - fore us___ and the road - side fire.
mp
37
40
mf
I will spin the sun - shine
cresc.
mf
42
cresc.
in - to gold - en thread, make a crown of___ moon - beams to place up - on your
cresc.
47
f
48
head. And this shall be for mu - sic___ when no one else is near, the
f

fine song for sing - ing, the rare song to hear. That
on - ly I re - mem - ber, that on - ly you ad - mire, of the
broad road be - fore us and the road - side fire. And
this shall be for mu - sic when no one else is near.

9. WHERE GO THE BOATS?

Words from A Child's Garden of Verses *by*
ROBERT LOUIS STEVENSON (1850-1894)

Music and additional Words by
MARY DONNELLY
and **GEORGE L. O. STRID**

2-part choral arrangement available (41738).

13
Bright green leaves a - float - ing, cas - tles of the foam,
17
boats of mine a - boat - ing, where will all come home?
21
mf
Where go the boats when they drift a - way, as off down the stream they go? And
25
mp
who will bring all my boats a - shore? I guess I'll nev - er know.
mf
mp

On goes the riv - er and
out past the mill, a - way down the val - ley, a-
way down the hill. A - way down the riv - er, a
hun - dred miles or more, oth - er lit - tle chil - dren shall

bring my boats a - shore. Where go the boats when they drift a - way, as
off down the stream they go? And who will bring all my boats a - shore? I
guess I'll nev - er know. I guess I'll
nev - er know.

10. THE WIND

Words *from* A Child's Garden of Verses *by*
ROBERT LOUIS STEVENSON (1850-1894)

Music by **MARY DONNELLY**
Arranged by **GEORGE L. O. STRID**

like la - dies' skirts a - cross the
grass.
O wind, a - blow - ing all day long,
O wind, that sings so loud a
song!
I

31
saw the dif - f'rent things you did,_____ but
35
you your - self you al - ways hid._____ I
39
felt you push,_ I heard you call,_____ I
43
could not see your - self at all. O

47
wind, a - blow - ing all day long,_______ O_
51
cresc.
wind, that sings so loud a song!_______
cresc.
decresc.
56 mf 57
O you that are so strong and cold,_______
mf
60
O blow - er, are you young or old?_______ Are

cresc. poco a poco
you a beast of field and tree, or just a strong - er
cresc. poco a poco
child than me? O wind, a - blow - ing
all day long, O wind, that sings so loud
a song!
8va

Robert Louis Stevenson (1850–1894) was a Scottish poet and novelist best known for his novels *Treasure Island, The Strange Case of Dr. Jekyll and Mr. Hyde,* and his book of poetry *A Child's Garden of Verses.*

Born and educated in Edinburgh, Scotland, Stevenson was the only child of Thomas Stevenson and Margaret Isabella Balfour. Robert and his mother were both prone to respiratory illness and fevers, and much of his early schooling was interrupted due to frequent sickness. He was taught by private tutors for extended periods of time, and became quite close with his nurse, Alison Cunningham, who cared for him through his many illnesses. Stevenson later dedicated *A Child's Garden of Verses* to her.

Interestingly, Stevenson was a late reader, not picking up the skill until he was seven or eight years old, but he frequently dictated stories to his mother and his nurse, and wrote stories throughout his childhood. His father, a lighthouse designer and engineer, was supportive of his writing, even paying for the publication of Robert's first book at age 16.

Stevenson studied law at Edinburgh University and qualified for the Scottish bar in 1875, but never actually practiced. Instead, he turned his efforts to travel and writing, soon making his way into an influential circle of London area writers. He moved a number of times in search of a climate more favorable to his health, but continued to struggle with illness for most of his adult life.

In 1880, Stevenson married Fanny Van de Grift Osbourne, a magazine writer and mother of two children. They continued to relocate frequently in the hopes of improving Stevenson's health, living in California, Great Britain, and the Adirondacks before ultimately settling in Samoa in the South Pacific. It was there that he died in December of 1894, after collapsing.

Stevenson's *A Child's Garden of Verses* has become a well-loved collection of poems about the imaginative life of children. Many of its poems have been set to music in the years since its publication. The themes of pretend play, curiosity, and joy transcend generations, and speak to the universal human experience.